IN AN EIGHTEENTH CENTURY KITCHEN

IN AN
EIGHTEENTH CENTURY
KITCHEN

A Receipt Book of Cookery
1698

=

Edited, with an Introduction, Notes and Glossary
BY DENNIS RHODES
a Preface
BY BEVERLEY NICHOLS
and illustrated
BY DUNCAN GRANT

=

CECIL WOOLF · LONDON

First published 1968
Reissued 1983

Cecil Woolf Publishers, 1 Mornington Place, London NW1 7RP
Tel: 01-387 2394

ISBN 0-900821-00-0

Preface

Since the publication of *A Thatched Roof*, in which the discovery of this volume is recorded, a third of a century has run its course, but my recollection of the event is still vivid. It was late on an October afternoon and we – my friend and I – had just come in from the garden. There were drifts of autumn crocuses in the orchard, the leaves were beginning to fall from the liquidambers, and, as we stepped into the music room, bending our heads to avoid the low beams of the old cottage, we were greeted by the pleasant fragrance of apple-smoke from the open grate. After a cup of tea, I was for exploring the garden again; flowers in the twilight are often even more beautiful than flowers at noon. But no, said my friend, we must explore the cottage instead; she was sure that there were still many secrets to be found. There were indeed; and this was one of them.

The cottage lay just outside the hamlet of Glatton in Huntingdonshire, and local records indicate that it was built in the latter part of the sixteenth century. Originally it had formed three cottages, but round about 1830 it was remodelled into a single unit, and to this date, presumably, we may attribute the narrow staircase that led to the three main bedrooms. Under this staircase was the little cupboard in which the Cookery Book was found. The walls had been often painted and repainted over the years, and it was only by chance that we noticed the cupboard at all. Having noticed it we obviously had to open it, and there was the book. How long it had lain there, whose hands had placed it there, we shall never know. But it says a great deal for the sturdy building of our forefathers that it was in such excellent condition, so little damaged by the passage of time.

The reader will perhaps forgive me if I recall, from *A Thatched Roof*, the emotions of a very young man:

Eagerly we leant over that book in the fading light – a golden October sunset that flooded onto the yellowing paper – yellow to yellow, with the grave black letters dancing before our eyes, as though they were overjoyed to be read again. As we turned the pages it seemed that there was a scent in the old room of ghostly sweetmeats; there drifted back to us the perfume of curious country wines, the aroma of forgotten preserves, the bitter-sweet flavour of kitchens which have long crumbled into dust.

This same aroma greets us as we open the present volume, which owes so much to the enthusiasm and the patient research of Dr. Dennis Rhodes. Although he has scrutinized the text with the eye of a scholar, he has turned the pages tenderly, keeping all the original spellings, dittographies, and errors. 'To have corrected them' he soberly observed 'would have been to spoil the character of the manuscript.' I would go further than that. To have corrected them would have been to rob the manuscript of its poetry, which sings through the titles with the sweetness of a lyric by Herrick or, for that matter, the label on a jar of country wine. There are phrases in this book – one of them is 'To Preserve Quinces Red or White' – which long to be set to music. There are others which evoke a whole social scene, a dance in an echoing barn, with the lady of the manor moving graciously among her tenants – 'To Make Slipcoat Chees. The Lady Bray's Recipe'. And others which might have set Hogarth's pencil wandering on the portrait of a country-woman – 'To Dry All Manner of Green Ploms'.

Although the book, of its very nature, is a period piece, the modern housewife would be very wrong if she were to imagine that it had no application to her own kitchen. It is as practical as any of the cookery columns in the Sunday newspapers. This I have proved for myself. If you have a liking for confectionery you will need to travel a long way before you find a better recipe than 'To Make Marchpane Paste', and it will taste all the sweeter because it is called by its pretty English name instead of being burdened by the ponderous Teutonic title 'marzipan'. You may not feel greatly drawn by 'Miss Leblanc's Receit to Stew Carp' – the

Preface

picture evoked by this phrase is somewhat intimidating – but you should certainly experiment with the Cowslip Wine. You will note that the flower is spelt three different ways, 'Couslep', 'Couslepe' and 'Couslip', and after three glasses of it they will all sound equally melodious. Miss Bruton's recipe 'To Stew a Rabit or a Hear' is thoroughly practical, and so is the one for Scotch Collops. And though I am not a snuff-taker I have the word of a Cambridge don that the 'snuffe' recommended in these pages is as potent and as pleasing as any that he ever sniffed, and was warmly received when he handed it round the High Table at Trinity College.

The romantic background to this small volume[1] – the manner of its finding, the nature of its contents, and the fact that now, after the lapse of centuries, it may make its unobtrusive way around the world – all these things are so obvious that they need not be stressed. Nor need we enlarge upon the staggering contrasts between the world in which it made its first appearance and the world in which it is published today. But I hope that the modern housewife, if she is kind enough to glance through it in her super-stream-lined kitchen, may spare a moment to reflect on those contrasts, and even to ask herself whether they are all in her favour – whether, indeed, this stream-lining may not have taken some of the spice out of life, and whether there may not perhaps be some connection between frozen food and frozen emotions.

BEVERLEY NICHOLS

[1] The original manuscript of 'A Receipt Book of Cookery' has now found a permanent home in the Hammond Museum, North Salem, Westchester, New York, which houses one of the world's most distinguished collections of the English domestic arts.

Introduction

—

The manuscript which is here edited and published in its entirety for the first time has been in the possession of Mr Beverley Nichols for over thirty years. How it came to light was told in his book *A Thatched Roof* which was first published in October 1933. The manuscript is on paper bearing an English watermark of the seventeenth century.[1] Writing in it has been begun in two places. A number of leaves have been torn out (when still blank, almost certainly) so that it is impossible to guess how many leaves the book originally contained. As it now stands, there is a title-leaf, then one blank leaf, then thirty-seven leaves bearing text; then come forty-one more blank leaves, followed by twenty-nine leaves bearing text, and finally eighty-one blank leaves, then several fragments where the leaves have been partially cut out with scissors, and at the end two more leaves bearing writing upside down, and one last blank leaf. The total number of extant complete leaves is thus 193, but only 69 of these are written on. There is no evidence that the twenty-nine written leaves in the second half of the book are later in writing than the written leaves at the beginning. The writing is usually on one side of the leaf only, but not always. The dates written in the manuscript range from 1698 on the title page to 1760 near the end. Clearly the majority of entries were written between 1700 and 1760. There is a variety of hands, and recipes were added at intervals. There are very few precise clues to the early ownership of the manuscript, but what few there are all suggest that it was kept in London. Written in red ink below the title are the initials F. B., which may indicate that the book belonged

---

[1] The watermark contains a coat of arms and sometimes the word COMPANY, which suggests that the paper was made by the Company of White Paper Makers, whose main activity in England was between 1686 and 1698. Thus the paper of the manuscript was quite new when the first owner wrote the title page in 1698.

to Fettiplace Bellers (1687-1750?), whose name appears towards the end of the text, or possibly to his mother, Frances Bellers, who died in 1716. The volume was clearly in the possession of the Bellers family for a time since it also contains the name of Mary Bellers: this may have been Fettiplace's wife, but we have no evidence that he was married. The facts here assembled concerning the life of Fettiplace Bellers are taken from the article on him by William E. A. Axon in the *Dictionary of National Biography* and from his own books, all of which are in the British Museum.

John and Frances Bellers were Quakers. John, a philanthropist, visited prisons and proposed that the prisoners should be 'treated with a dinner of baked legs and shins of beef and ox cheeks; which is a rich and yet cheap dish, with which they may be treated plentifully for 4d a head, or less'. Did John Bellers know of the recipes in this book? He probably knew some of them from his wife, but he need not have seen the actual volume which we have here. John and Frances had one son, Fettiplace, who was born in the parish of St. Andrew's, Holborn, London, in 1687. John died in 1725, aged about seventy-one. Fettiplace wrote an anonymous play called *Injur'd Innocence, a tragedy*, which was acted at Drury Lane in February 1732 and printed in the same year. It was, however, a failure. A work entitled *Of the Ends of Society* was drawn up in 1722 but did not appear until 1759. His most important work is *A Delineation of Universal Law : being an Abstract or Essay towards deducing the Elements of Natural Law from the First Principles of Knowledge and the Nature of Things. In five books*. This work, on which he laboured for twenty years, was printed for Dodsley in 1750. The 'Advertisement' shows that it was a posthumous publication; there was a second edition in 1754 and a third in 1759. The advertisement printed in 1750 distinctly states that Bellers was dead, yet the official archives of the Royal Society record that he was elected a fellow on 30 November 1711, was admitted on 17 April 1712, and withdrew from the society on 12 April 1752. This chronological puzzle, as Axon remarks, remains unsolved, and unfortunately the page which appears in our manuscript in Bellers' handwriting is undated and so does not help.

The other people named in the manuscript, mainly women, are unidentifiable. One of them at least tells us that he was writing in London. Cookery books have always been immensely popular in England. The reader will obtain an excellent introduction to their history from William Carew Hazlitt's *Old Cookery Books and Ancient Cuisine*, London, 1886. Some of the most important books published during the period with which we are here concerned, and which have been useful to me in editing the text are the following:

1   *The True Way of Preserving & Candying, and Making several sorts of sweet-meats, according to the best & truest manner. Made Publick for the benefit of all English Ladies and Gentlewomen; especially for My Schollars.* pp. 154. London, Printed for the Author, in the year, 1681. (The author of this book is unknown.)

2   Henry Howard, *England's Newest Way in all sorts of Cookery, Pastry, and all pickles that are fit to be used.* London, 1710.

3   *A Collection of above Three Hundred Receipts in Cookery, Physick and Surgery, for the use of all good wives, tender mothers, and careful nurses.* By several hands. pp. 218. London, 1714.

4   *Mrs Mary Eales's Receipts.* London, 1718 (Another edition, 1733.)

5   Mary Eales, *The Compleat Confectioner; or, the art of candying and preserving.* London, 1733.
   Mrs Eales is described as 'late confectioner to her late Majesty Queen Anne'.

6   John Nott, *The Cook's and Confectioner's Dictionary: or, the Accomplish'd Housewife's Companion. Revised and recommended by John Nott, Cook to his Grace the Duke of Bolton.* London, 1723.
   John Nott has a chapter entitled 'To make Quiddany of Rasberries', and another on 'Apricock Jumbals', in

which he writes 'Colour it with Cochineal or Saunders'.
(See Glossary.)

7 E. Smith, *The Compleat Housewife: or, Accomplished Gentlewoman's Companion*. First edition, 1727; second edition, 1728; third edition, 1729.

Very little is known about E. Smith; for instance, it is not known whether or not she was married; but it is believed that her name was probably Elizabeth. The first and second editions of her book are rare enough not to be in the British Museum. The work was enormously popular and went through many editions. She has a chapter entitled 'To mumble Rabbets and Chickens'.

8 Charles Carter, *The Compleat City and Country Cook*. London, 1732.

9 Vincent La Chapelle (chief cook to the Rt Hon the Earl of Chesterfield), *The Modern Cook*. 2 vols. London, 1733.

10 *The Young Lady's Companion in Cookery and Pastry, Preserving, Pickling, Candying, &c*. Written by a Gentlewoman who formerly kept a Boarding School. pp. 204. London, 1734. This contains a chapter 'To make Quidney of Rasberries'.

11 Finally there is one of the best and most successful of all cookery books, the first edition of which came out anonymously in 1747: *The Art of Cookery made plain and easy*. By a Lady. [By Hannah Glasse.]

There were many successive editions. The book has been useful in editing the present manuscript, and it seems probable that a copy of it was in the hands of at least some of our owners. Mrs Glasse included the section on the bite of a mad dog by Dr Richard Mead, and it may be that this was copied out of her book into our manuscript after 1747.

In transcribing the text I have decided rigorously to preserve all the original spellings, chaotic and erratic though these may be, and to keep all dittographies and other obvious errors as they are found in the manuscript. To have corrected them would have been to spoil the character of the manuscript, which is a compilation in different hands by a number of persons (probably mainly women) of differing degrees of literacy. It is possible to detect, when the handwriting changes from one person to another, a rise or a fall in the knowledge of spelling on the part of the writer. To have standardised this inconsistency would have been to ruin the nature of a typical eighteenth-century scrap-book written by a group of non-academic people. It may be noted in conclusion that when one compares this with the books described above and published between 1700 and 1750, one is immediately struck by the differences in literary presentation. While the manuscript is full of errors and inconsistencies, the printed books are remarkably accurate and consistent, particularly in spelling, and give the appearance of being much more modern in composition. Their publishers probably subjected them to a process of polishing before printing, but at the same time one must admit that they were written by authors with a higher level of scholarship behind them than our simple cooks. Only Fettiplace Bellers can claim any kind of a literary position.

I have added textual notes at the end of the text, and made a glossary of difficult or obsolete words which need explanation.

D.E.R.

PART ONE

Part One

———

From Ye Lady Jepheris

To Preserve Walnuts

Take your walnuts y^e first full moon after midsummer, before they come to have any shell, and boil them in severall waters to take away y^e bitterness, but let ye first water still boil before you shift ye nuts into it, and while they are hot peel off ye thin skin, then take their wait or somwhat more of good Loaf Shuger, and put some water to it then set it on ye fire, and when it is scumd, put in the nuts to ye sirip, also 2 or 3 cloves and a nutmeg quartred, tie it up in a Little lawn, so let them boyl gently at first, for they will take ye shuger ye better, then quicken ye fire and boil it up and keep it for your use.

To Preserve Goosberys

Take 3 quarters of a pound of fair goosberys wth out spots or specks, take their weight in double refin'd shuger before they are slit, or the seeds are taken out, & y^n take y^m and slit y^m down ye sem^1, & take out all ye seeds, & cut a little of ye stock & ye Eye of y^m but not all, & break your suger in 2 or 3 pices, & just dip all ye pices into some clean water, and put it in ye scillet & break it, if it sucked not water enough in dipping, put in a spoonfull or 2 of water more, and set it over some clean wodcoles or charcole, when it is boylt, scum it and put in ye goosberys, & there let y^m boyl and they will be soon done.

From Ye Lady Lewcy's Woman

To Make Sugar Cakes

Take double refin'd Sugar wet it with faire water, Set it over the fire & boil it to a Suger again, then have ready the Juse of Rasberys of Currents, or what frute you like, & put soe much as w^ll just wet ye Sugar set it over a soft fire till ye Sugar be meled,[2] let it but just boil & then drop it upon plates or glasses, you must first strew sugar upon the plates Jilliflowers violets you must infuse them in water for sorrol or sage or any green thing put the juse.

To Preserve Apricoks 17..[3]

Take fairest and largest apricocks, open ye sem[1] side, & take out the stones, pare them and thake their weight in sugar, then put y^m in a clean stone pot, and cover them up all night wth ye sugar upon them, next day put in as much water as will melt ye sugar, then put in the apricocks, Lett y^m boil verry leasurely, when it w^ll jelly in a spoon it is enough, put y^m into a glass cover them not till they be coold.

Idem

To Preserve Pipins Green

Take apint of ye liquour made of pipins and John Apples a pound of pipins pared, and take their weight in Sugar, when ye liquor hath boild a little scuming it well, put in your pipins & make them boil verry fast, take off ye scum as it riseth, now and then strow some fine beaten sugar upon them to keep them whole, you must have Lemon or oring pill[4] cut in little peices, & boild very well & tender to put in your syrrup, & when they look green then they are enough, put in as much Juce of Lemmons as you think fitt, & let it boil a little, let them boil before you glass them.

To Preserve Cheries in Gelly

Take 2 pints of Conduit water, one pound of codlings, pare and quarter them, one pound of well colloured cherries Ston'd at Scalck'd,[5] then cruch them into the codlngs and water, set them on the fire, Let them boyl very fast, scum them and when you think they are half boyld away, put it through a Ceive, put into the liquor 1 pound and $\frac{1}{2}$ of fine sugar & 1 pound of y^e fairest Cerries, Lett y^m seeth to gether like a peice of beef, if it Jellies put y^m into the glasses, put y^e Cherries first and then pour in y^e Jellie.

4

Martha Benthall

To Make Cowslep Wine

Take 7 gallons of water put in as much Sugar as w[ll] make it
so strong as it w[ll] bear an Egg, set it on y[e] ffire till it w[ll] be
clear that no Scum w[ll] arise, so let it stand untel it be but
blood warm, so poure it on 2 Pecks of couslep pips, then put
in 4 Lemons cut peell and all in, then let it stand wth a
quarter or half of a pint of good lite yest, for to work, then let
it stand a day & a night, then strain out the Cowleps, then
put y[e] Lemons into y[e] barrell, then let it stand about 2 weeks
before you bottle it.

To Make Diet Bread

Take eight eggs both yolks and whites, & beat them I[6] a
beason or wooden boul a quarter of an houre, then put to
them a pound of sugar, & beat them together as long again,
then put in to them a pound of fine flower, and a quarter of
an ounce of Aneseeds, Caraway seeds, and beat them to
gether while your oven is heating, and when it is as hot as for
Manchet, then butter your pans or pleats, and put it into
them, and when you pleas you may draw it and keek it for
your use.

To Make Sugar Plate
to Print in Mouls or
to Make any Artificial Frutes or
Muscardine Comfits

Take a small quantity of gum dragaunt, and Lay it in steep
in rosewater till it is desolved into a gelly, then strain it
through a Cloth & beat it in a morter, till it looks very white,
then put some searced sugar Into it, & beat it together, &
when you have beaten it wth somuch searsed sugar y[t] it is so
stif, y[t] you may take it out of yo[r] Morter, take it forth & work
it into a stif paste wth searsed sugar, so you may print it in yo[r]
mouls or use it other wise, as you please.

To Make White or Red Muscardine Comfits to Granish a Marchpane

Take your sugar plates & work y^m as thin as you can and in them some musk, Then wth a jaging Iron in ye manner of Losinges & dry y^m & keep y^m for yor use, Then if you w^{ll} have y^m red, work a little Rosset or Saunders Into your paste & so Roule it out and use them as you do yor White ones.

To Candy Flowers

Take gum Arraback & lay it in steep in rose water till it is desolved then take white sugar Candy & bruse it very small then take your flowers in ye heat of ye day & lay them upon ye bottom of a Sive & wet them over wth ye gum water & strow ye sugar candy upon them & set them into ye Sun to dry & as they doe dry put off ye sugar Candy upon them & when ye one side of them is dry & candied then turn them & candey ye other sid of them in ye same manner & so use them as your pleas.

To dry Pears

Take Small ale wort & sweeten a quarte of it wth a pint of honey and put so many pears as your wort w^{ll} cover & let them boyl in it till they are very tender then lay them upon ye bottome of a Sive & put them into a hot oven & so dy^7 them for your use.

To Dry all Manner of Green Ploms

Take any kind of green ploms & Scald them in hot watter & peele ye thine Skin off from them, then put them into ye Same watter againe & cover them close & lett them Stand over a Soft fire & they will turne very green againe, & when they are very green clarifie a pound of Sugar & boyle it to a full Surrup & put three quarters of a pound of plomes into it & lett them boyle very leasurely untile they are so tender that you may feele ye Stones of them, then take them forth of ye Sirrupp & dust them over wth Searsed Sugar & lay them upon a pye plate & so dry them for your Use.

To Dry Pippins

Take old pippins & pare them & cut them In halfs & take y^e
Coars out of them, then clarifie a pound of sugar & boil it to
a full Sirrup & put somany pippins into it as yor sirrup w^{ll}
cover & let them boyl very fast till they are so tender y^t you
may put a straw through them y^n take them forth & dust
them over wth searsed sugar & lay them uppon a py plate &
dry them and keep them for yor use.

To Dry Cherries or Grapes

Take your Cherries or Grapes & pricke them full of holes wth
a Small pine[8] & dust them over wth Searsed Sugar then lay
them upon the bottome of a Sive & after you have drawne
forth any bread out of ye Oven put your Cherryes or Grapes
into it & Cover ye Oven close & once in a quarter of an hour
dust them over wth Searsed Sugar for ye Space of three houers
& So lett them Stand in it till they are through[9] dry, then put
them up in Boxes & keep them for your use.

To Clarifie Sugar

Take a Pint of Faire water & beat ye white of an Ege in it to a
Froath then put a pound of Sugar into it & Set it to boyle &
there will rise a blacke Skum upon ye top of your Sugar & as
ye Skum doth rise take it of very clean & Straine it through a
Cloth & it will looke very clear & So you may use it as you
please.

To Boile Sugar
to a thine Sirrup

After your Sugar is clarified Set it to boile againe & as there
did rise a blacke Skum upon ye top of your Sugar in y^e
Clarifying of it, So there will rise a Second Skum upon it w^{ch}
will be very white, & as ye Skum doth rise take it off very
cleane, & when it will deliver no more Skum, then it is in a
thin Sirrup & will be very clear, but it will look white & pale
coullered & So you may use it as you please.

To Boile Sugar to a Full Sirrup

When your Sugar is boiled to a full Sirrup it will looke high coullered of ye Couller of Amber or Strong bear,[10] & So you may use it as you please.

To Preserve Green Apricocks or Almonds

Take your apricocks or Almonds when ye stones of them are so soft y^t you may put a pin through them y^n scald them in hot water & take ye scurf from them y^n put them in ye same water again and let them stand over a soft fire till they are green again then clalifi a pound of Sugar & boy[11] it to a full sirrup & put half a pound of Apricocke or Almonds into it & let them boy leasurely till they are very tender y^n let them Coole & so keep them for your use.

To Preserve Orringes or Lemons

Take yor orringes & lemons & cut in halves & take ye meat out of them y^n take ye meat out of them y^n take yor Orringes or Lemons & lay them 3 days in water shifting them once a day y^n Clarifie a pound of Sugar & boyl it to a thin sirrup and boyl your Orrings or Lemons in fair water till they be very tender y^n put them into ye Sirrup & let them boyl til yor sirrup be boyld to a full sirrup & put them up and keep them for use.

To Know When Sugar is Boiled to a Manus Christie Heighte

It will then draw between your Fingers like a Small thread & So you may use it as you please.

When Boiled to a Candy Height

When Sugar is boiled to a Candy height it will draw between your Fingers in great Flackes like berdlime & So you may use it as you please.

When Boiled to a Casting Height

After ye Sugar is clarified Set it to boile againe till it is Somthing thicke, then Stir it wth a Sticke & Somtimes Swing your Stick from you & when it is boiled to a Casting height it will draw between your Fingers in great Flackes like Fethers or like great Flackes of Snow Flying in ye Ayre & So you may use it as you please.

To Make Prime Biscackes

Take six eggs both yolks and white and beat them In a bason or woden boul a quarter of an houre, then put to them a pound of fine flower & a quarter of an ounce of Ainseds or Caraway seeds, & beat them well together while your oven is a heating, & when it is hot as for Manchet, butter your pans and put it into y^m, & backe it, and when it is could you may keep it and dry it for your use.

To Make Almond Cake

Take half a pound of Almonds and blanch them, & beat them very small wth rose water, then put to them half a pound of fine flower a pound of Sugar, & ye whites of four eggs, & beat them together while your oven heats & when it is hot as for Manchet, butter your papers & lay them upon them, and beak them, and keep them and dry them, & keep for your use.

To Make Marchpane Paste

Take a pound of Almonds & blanch them, and beat them to mash In a Morter, then put half a pound of Sugar to them, and beat them together an houre, and it w^{ll} be in a paste, and if you see your paste beat Oylie put into it a little Rose water, & beat it together and that w^{ll} take away the Oyliness from it, and so you may print it in your moulds, make a Machpane wth it, or use it other wise as you please.

To Make Naples Bisket

Take 3 Egs both Yolkes & Whites, & beat them in a bason, or wooden Bowle a quarter of an hour, then put to them halfe a pound of Sugar, & beat them together as longe againe, then put to them 6 Ounces of fine flower & a graine or 2 of muske, being Steeped in a Spoonfull or two of Rosewater, & beat

9

them well together while your Oven is a heating, & when it is as hot as for Manchett, butter your pans, & put your bread into them & backe it, & dry it, & keep it for your Use.

To Dry Cherryes or Grapes

Take your Cherreys or grapes & prick them full of holes wth a small pin & dust them over wth searc'd sugar y^n lay them upon ye bottome of a sive and after you have draun forth bread out of ye oven put your Cherreyes or Grapes into it & covever ye Oven close & once in a quarter of an houre dust them over wth searced sugar for ye space of 3 howers & so let them to stand in it till they are throughly dry, y^n put them up in a box and keep them for your use.

To Make White Marmelate of Quinces

Take your quinces & pare them cut them in quarters & strain them through a suive or a Clean Cloath then take a pound of double refined sugar & clarifie it & set it to boyl & while it boyleth, take a pound and a half of your quinces & dry them in a platter over a Chafing dish of coals & when yor sugar is boyled to a Casting heigh put yor quinces into it & stir it well together over ye fire & then put it into your boxes & keep for your use.

To Make Red Marmelate of Qunces

Take yor quinces & pare them & cut the meat from ye coars in thin slices y^n Clarifie a pound of Sugar & put a pound of quinces into it and cover it close & let it boyl very leasurely till yor quinces are red y^n uncover it & let it boyl very fast keeping it stiring till it comes clear from ye bottome of yor pan y^n put it in boxes & keep it for your use.

To Make Quodeny of any Kind of Plumes

Take any kind of plomes & boyl them all to peices in Apple water y^n strain ye water from them again & put to a pint of ye said water a quarter of a pound of Loaf Sugar & let it boyl till it hangs thick at your spoon then wet yor moulds & put it into them and when it is through could ^{12} put it into boxes and keep it for your use.

To Make White or Red Quodeny of Pipins

Take yor pipins & cut them to pices & put to them as much fair water as w^{ll} cover them & boyl them all to pices then strain ye water from them & put to a pint of ye said water a quarter of a pound of Loaf sugar & if you w^{ll} have it to be white boyl it very fast uncovered & if you w^{ll} have it red boyl it very leasurely till it looks read y^n uncover it and let boyl uncovered till it hanges thick at your spoon y^n wet yor moulds & put it into them & when it is through could^{12} put it into boxes keep it for your use.

To Make Paste of Pipins

Take yor pipins & pear them, then cut them in halfs & boyl them very tender in fair water y^n clarifi a pound of sugar & boyl it to a casting height and put a pound of pipins into it & keep it stiring till it comes clean from ye bottome of ye Skillet then lay it upon plates & dry it & keep it for yor use.

To Make Paste of Quinces

Take yor quinces & pare them & boyl them very tender in fair water & strain them through a sive y^n Clarifie a pound of sugar and boyl it to a candy height & put a pound of quinces into it and keep it stiring over ye fire till it comes clean from ye bottome of yor pan y^n lay it upon plates & dry it and keep it for your use.

To Make Paste of Apricocks

Take yor Apricocks being full ripe & put them into a pot & cover it close & set them into a kettle of water & let them boyl very leasurely till they are very tender y^n let them cool & 3 days after poure ye liquor clean from them & as it doth boyl take ye white of an egg & beat it in fair water to a froth & put ye froth into ye surrup & y^t w^{ll} make it look vrey clear again y^n put it to yor Apricocks again when it is very clear & so keep them for your use.

To Make Past of Orringes or Lemons

Take ye peeles of your Orringes or Lemons & boyle them very tender in faire Water & Straine them through a Sive then put to halfe a pound of your Orringe or Lemon halfe a pound of ye pulp of pippins then Clarifie a pound of Sugar & boyle it to a Candy height & put your pulpe into it, & keep it Stiring till it comes cleane from ye bottome of your pan then lay it upon plates & dry it & keep it for your Use.

To Make Paste of Barbaries

Take a pound of ye pap of pipins & strain as much of ye juse of barberies into it till it looks very red y^n clarifie a pound of Sugar & boyl it to a Casting height & put yor pulp into it & keep it stiring till it comes clean from ye bottome of your pan y^n lay it upon plates & dry it & keep it for your use.

To Make Paste of all Manner of Plums

Take yor plums being full ripe & put them into a pot and cover them cloase and set them into a kettle of water & let them boyl y^n strain them throug a sive & put to half a pound of ye pulp of pipins half a pound of yor plums then strain them through a clean cloth both together y^n clarifie a pound of Sugar & boyl it to a Casting height & put yor pulp into it & keep it stiring over ye fire till it comes clean from ye bottome of yor pan y^n lay it upon plates & dry it & keep it for yor use.

To Preserve Cherreys to Keep in a Quacking Jelley all ye Winter

Take a pound of Sugar & Clarifie it & boyl it to a casting height y^n put a pound & a halfe of Cherryes into it & let them boyl very faste & ye juce of yor cherryes w^{ll} turn yor shirrup thin again but yet keep them sill boyling till ye sirrup hangs at your spoon y^n set them to Cool & ye sirrup of them will be quaking jelley & so you may use them as you pleas.

To Preserve Damsons

Take a pound of sugar & Clarifie it & Boy it to a full surrup & put a pound of yor Damsons into it & lett them boyl very leasurely till they are very tender y^n set them to coole & 3 day after pour ye sirrup from them and put half a pint of Apple water into it & boyl it by it's self till it is boyled to a quacking jelly & take ye scum off from it y^n put it to yor Damsons again boyling hot & so keep them for your use.

To Preserve Quinces Red

Take a pound of sugar & clarifie it & put a pint of Apple water into it & boyl it till it is in a full sirrup y^n put three quarters of a pound of quinces into it & cover it cloas & let them boyl very leasurely till they are so tender y^t you may put a straw through them then take them forth and boy ye sirrup by it self till itis in a quacking Jelley y^n set them to Cole & put it to your quinces again & keep them for your use.

To Preserve Quinces White

Take your quinces & parboyl them very tender in fair water y^n pare them & cover them y^n clarify a pound of sugar & boyl it to a full sirrup & put 3 quarters of a pound of quinces into it & boyl them somthing leasurly uncovered till they are so tender y^t you may put a straw through them y^n take them forth of ye sirrup & put half a pint of Apple water into it & boyl it by its self till it is in a quacking jelley y^n put it to your quinces again & keep them for yor use y^n if yor surrup is too red make a new sirrup for them of Apple water & boyl it very fast & put them to it & make quodiny of ye first sirrup.

To Preserve Barbaries

Take a pint of Apple water & boyl a pound of Sugar in it till it is well desolved then take half a pound of barberies & stone them and put them into ye sirrrup and let them boyl very fast till the sirrup is in a quacking jelley then set them to coole & keep them for your use.

To Preserve Gren Figs or Lattice Stalcks

Take fair water & make it into a strong brine y^t it w^{ll} bear an eg on ye top of it y^n put yor lattice stalcks & divid yor brine into 2 parts put your stalcks into one par & yor figs into ye other & let them lie in it 3 days y^n boyl them tender in fair water y^n clarifie a pound of Sugar & boyl it to a thin sirrup and put a pound of yor figs of stalcks into it & let them boyl untill yor sugar be in a full sirrup y^n let them cool and keep them for yor use.

To Preserve Grapes

Take a pound of Sugar & Clarifie it & boyl it to a full Sirrup y^n take half a pound of grapes & prick them full of holes wth a Small pin & put them into your sirrup & put them into a gelley pot & set it into a Skillet of water & let them boy[1] in it till they are very tender y^n set them to cole & keep them for yor use.

To Make Couslip Wine Very Good

Take 3 gallans of water put it to 6^{lb} of lofe sugar boyle it to gather half an hower or beter w^n ye scum ariseth take it of & y^n power it into a earthen steane scolding-hot to your gallen of picked couslips w^n it is most could[13] take a spunfull of yeale est[14] beat it well with 18 sponfuls of serrup of citturn or lemon if it can be got bruing it togather with a dish very well well with ye liquear & let them work for to or three days y^n strain it forth & w^n it have done working over stop it close & in three weks or a month bottle it up puting into every bottle a lump of sugar cork it close.

To Make Egg Wine Very Plesent & Good to Cole ye Back & to Strengthen it

Take a quart of water & half a pint of Renish win & the whits of six eggs a nutmeg cut in quarters 4 bige peces of lemond pill a sprig of rosmery sweten it with fine lofe suger to your tast breew all togather for an houer strain it throw a straining bagg & y^n botle it up don[15] . . .

To Preserve Apricoks

Take your apricoks y^t be not over ripe & pare y^n & cut y^m in rasnoble[16] thin slises but not to were the stone[17] y^n. way y^m & to every pound put a quarter of a pound of ye best duble refind sugar y^n take of ye water of green Codlings so much as you coseve[18] w^{ll} boyle y^m to gely with ye waight of your water in sugar put your apricocs & water & sugar togather in a skilut over a very quick fier only Resarving a little of your sugar to put to y^m in the boyling & w^n your apricocs grow clere they are sufficeant.

To Make Corrant Wine

Let your corrant be very ripe before you gather y^m in a dry day & tow 3 pounds of corrants put one pound of sugar of 5^d the pound & a quart of water & so way your corrants & mesure your water & put both water & corrants into a woden tray or any such thing & breake the frut very well with your hand y^n strain them through a hair sive y^n put the sugar to it & put it up into a runlet or any vesels & when you have fill it up y^n let it work as long as it will before you stop it up then let it stand tow Months or a quartor of a year if you please but 2 Months is anough befor you bottle it.

To Make Marmalet of Apricocks

Take apricocks pare them & slice y^m very thin & double refind sugar then boile it to a cadi[19] then put y^m togather & boyle it & skim it & put it in glaces don . . .

To Make Slipcoat Chees   the Leady Bray

Take on galan[20] of the stroakings of your kind[21] & put into it a quart of water hot enough to warm ye milk so run it as you would any other chees w^n it is come fill your Pale without braking it at all & let it sink in of it self without crushing it with your hand neiter pres it at all for the first & second day as oft as you find the chees clothes wet you must turn it into a dry one the third day you must take it out of the cloth & let it ly thereupon turn it into fresh gras & wipe it & turn it many times a day changing or turning the gras every day an so order it tell you eat it if the wether be cold you may cover it with a cloth upon the grass.

To Preserve Orinmges

First waigh your Orinmges & take their waight in double refind Sugar y^n litly & finly great y^m all over y^n boyle them in spring water tell they are tender y^n cut of a litle of the top to the bignes of sixpence pick out what seds you cane y^n have ready boyled a litle water & sugar to put y^m in to be there a little boyld again whilst you make a pint of piping gelly to every Pound off sugar put a pint piping liquer y^n put in ye orinmges w^n tis half boyld to a gelley y^n boyle up the orinmges & all tell it be quite a gelly y^n glas up the orinmges & keep a litle gely to cover ye orinmges w^n cold we never do but on[22] oring at a time.

To Pickle Walnuts

Take the Walnuts & Put y^m into Some Cold Water and Set them over the fire tell they are Scalding hot Then take y^m off and Let y^m Stand tell you can rub off the outside thin Skin Then take some brine Strong Enough to bare an Egge and Put them into, and Shift y^m every every Day for nine Days togather, Then take too 2 Gallons of the Best White Wine Vineger & Quarter of an Ounce of Cloves and an Ounce of Race-Ginger of Jamaica Pepper and Black Pepper take half an Ounce of each half an ounce of Whole White Pepper a Quarter of an Ounce of Nutmegs 2 Penny Worth of Mace boyl all then wth the Vinegar a Quarter of an hour then add to every gallon of the Pickle a Good Spoonfull of Mustard Seed Beat and Sifted & three Cloves of Garlick, This must be put in when it is cold and the Walnuts Draind Dry from the Brine.

Sarah Lovedays Receit to Make Metheglin

Boyle the water with the Herbs which is roosmary and sweet margerum then strain it out & let it stand tell it is Almost Could then put in the hunny there should be a pound of hunny to a quart of water it must be mixt well together then put it into the kettell & let it boil up & scum it well then put in some bruised sinament[23] & ginger & let it boyle a Littel then strain it of & when it is almost Could work it for 2 or 3 days let it stand for a quarter of a Year before its tapt.

To Make Snuffe

Take 2 Ounces of bestt Tobacco 2 Nutmegs of Sweett marjorum Rosemary Germandor Bittony & Bassille thimee one handfulle pound all these welle together & pouder them Very fine & youse it for Snushe.

To Pickle Pidgeons   Ann Mills

Take the Largestt young Pidgeons pulle & Crap them draw them then bone & Lard them with bakin[24] in the Inside then take pickled Coucumbers & Capers & aboutt 2 Anchovies to half a dozen pidgeons & Season itt with Cloves & Mace & Nutmegg Saltt & Little peper with a Little Small time & green marjorum then Shred all these togather & Stuff their Insides with these pickles butt nott to fulle then tye up their necks with a thread besure nott to Break the scins not theyer guts with Boaning nor make to bigg a hole att their necks in Crapping make the pickle with the Bones of the Pidgeon & the Livers & Gissards & pinions & a poar pidggion if[25] have one the Pickle mustt be made of water & Vinegar & seasoned with Saltt & hole Peper a few hole Cloves scum the pickle when itt Boyles & then Putt in the Pidgion to Boyle in itt they wille be boyled in half an hour or Less then take them up & keep them tille they are cold & scum the pickle when Cold to take of the Fatt then putt them in & kep for use.

A Drink for a Horses Colde   R Kirton

Take a Handfulle of Feather few a Little Handfulle of Rue, Two or 3 Spoonfulls of Anneseeds, Boyle these in 3 pints of Ale Then putt in 2 or 3 Spoonfulls of horse Spice, the Quantity of an Egg of hoggs Larde If dangerous putt the Quantity of a Walnutt of horse Allawaye Sweten itt with a Little Treakle or hony & give itt the Horse Luke warm.

17

AQUA MIRABILIS

Take a drachm & the weightt of six pence of Cubebs so much more Labdamum as much Gallingall, of mace ginger & nutmegg a Like Quentity, of orange Lemon & Elecampagn of Each on dram Mellelott Flowers & Rosemary Flowers of Each a drachm & the weightt of sixpence all these mustt be beaten into gross powder & putt into a Quartt of white wine wth a Pinte of the Iuce of Spermintt & Balme one pinte of Aqua Vitae, so lett itt Stand twenty four hairs[26] then putt itt into a Close Still with a Quartt of white wyne more wash the glass.

Dr BROOKES CORDIAL

Take 2 Gallons of good Brandy & 4 of Spring Watter & cut into it 12 Bunches of wormwood 12 of mint & 12 Baeme[27] & as much Cardus in Weight as one of ye 12 Bunches & let them Stand 2 Days & nights Close Covered in an Earthen Pan Turning ye Hearbs Sometimes and then Still it in a Lymbeck pasted up & draw of 4 Gallons of watter & Mix ye watter all together & to every Point of Water put in an Ounce & half of Single refind Sugar you may put in about 3 Bunches of Rew

YEAR MISS LEBLANC RECEIT TO STEW CARP 1750

Take your Carps scale & rub them well with Salt then cut them in the nape of the neck & round the tail to make them bleed ; cut up the Belly take out the liver and guts take heed you do not break the gall then take one Spoonfull of Vinegar and rub them with & Save that Liquor to mix with your gravy then put them in a Stew pan with their Blood one half gravy and the other half vine enough to cover them a piece of Butter as larg as an Egg an onion with six cloves stuck in it two blad of mace D^oz pepper Corns, & a bunch of Sweet-herbs then Stew them half an hour of one side then turn and Stew them half an hour of the other side.

then take out your Carp and herbs and thicken the Sauce with Burnt Butter then put in your Carp and Serve it up with fry^d Bread and the row

1752 Mʳˢ POWELL WAY. TO COLLER BEEF

Take a middle Briskett of Beefe & Bone it & beat it with a Roaling pin, but not so much as to brake the fatt, if it be a larg peas of Beefe Take two ounces of salt Peter if a lettle peice one ounces will do, rub it very well in it & let it lye four days, Turning it Twice a day Then season it well with pepper salt mace & nuttmeg, & sage Thyme & parsley Then roal it up very hard in a Cloth & tye it round with beggars tape as hard as you can, let your pan be long enough for the Beef to lye down in, Then put half a pint of red port Three or four Spoonfull of gravey the rest water enough to Cover it Bake it with Bronw Bread you must put a Bunch of sweet herbs & one onion put also a little salt in your liquor Tye a string to the end of your Coller & hang it up uppon a hook 'till Cold then put it into your pickle with the Cloth on, & as you cut it keep it Tyed down.

TO STEW OYESTER

Plump Them in There owne liquor after They are washed in it & Straned then sett on the oyester liquor some white Vine a little whole peper a Blade of mace let it boil well Then Clap in your oyesters & Thicken Them with The yolk's of Two Eggs & a peas of Butter worked with a little flower & put some sippets under Them.

1752
MRS POWELL WAY TO MAKE BLUMMONGE

Take an ounce of Isingglass & a pint of Spring water & a stick of Cinnomon & boil it til it comes to 3 spoonfull, Then Strain it Take a Quart of Cream & boil it, put nine or ten better Almonds, blanched & beaten Then put the Isingglass Almonds & Cream Togather & boil it 'Till it is very Thick sweeten it to your Tast & put some orange flower water in before the Almonds, when boiled anough stain[28] it into little Chine Cups not full; when Turned out slice some Cittron & orange peel & Stick on Them I belive The Cups must be wet with Cold water.

1752 Mrs Powell Way To Make a Trifle

Take savoy biskakes dip Them in sack & lay Them in the
bottom (allmost double) of a Cheney dish Then Take a pint
of Cream & make a custard with four eggs boil The Custard
& pour it on The bistcakes: Then Take a pint of Cream &
make a whipt sillybub & put it on the Custard.
N.B. when you eat it put your spoon into The Bottom of The
dish.

1752 Mrs Powell Way Beefe Alamode

Take a leg of beefe bone it & mince The flesh Then put it into
a morter & beate it well Then season it with a little peper &
some nutmegg mace cloues & salt & lay it into a pott with a
buch of sweet herbs & beate all the Bones in peices & lay at
The Tope of your seasoned meate & set it into an Oven with
Brown Bread when its baked Take out The meate & put it
into another pott pressing The meate Clowns putting out The
grauy This must be done when The meate is hott and Then
melt up The marrow & if There be not enough to cover The
meate put some butter to it & poure it on The meate Till it is
covered.

Sauce for Three Boyld Chicknes

Mix One Spoonfull of Viniger. 2 or 3 of Water $\frac{1}{2}$ an Anchove
a Little thyme a Little Lemon peal & a Nutmeg Simmer it
oft & with this Liquor melt the butter as thick as you can,
boile 3 Eggs very hard leave out the White of One chop them
very Small & a Little Parsley with them & some lemmon peal
chop them very fine & put them altogether in the butter is
melted let them have a Shake or two over the fire, & put
your Chickens in the Dish & pour the Sauce over them.

To Make the Bath Cakes

Take a half a pound of fine flower put in it Nine Spoonfulls of
new Yest, that is not bitter, Nine Eggs leave out four of the
whites then put in two Spoonfulls of Brandy, wherein has
been Steept some Saffron, Set this by the fire to rise, & when

it is pufft up, then take One pound of Butter beat to Cream & mix with it One pound of fine flower, then put them altogether, & take One pound of carryway comfits & mingle them in, keeping some out to Strow over the top, & bake them uppon tin plates, drop them about the Size of halfpenny Wiggs.

To Make a Shaking Puding

Take a pint Cream & boyle mace in it a little nutmeg a little ginger then beate half a quarter of a pound of Almons with a little Rosewater, beat 4 Eggs 2 whites & Straine all these with the Crame togeather then put in Som grated bread, salt & sugar So mingle them well then take a thick cloth & rub it well with flower & tye it up & put it into Scathing water & boyle it, then when it is boyld melt some butter with 2 Spoonfulls of white wine or rosewater which you please & beat it well & sweeten it with Sugar, So Sarve it.

To Fatt Chicken

Take Barley meal & fine bran, not sifted to Clean about an Equall quantity & mix it with sume scim milk or milk & water & let Them drink scim milk or milk & watter, about Ten day or a fornight will fatt Them.
Take care they haue not The pip under The Tonge.

Sauce for Fish

Take three anchoves mince Them very samll a bitt of Horse Radish a bit onion & Lemon peel a little whole peper & some Time Then put in the Juce of one lemon or some Vinger & let Those stand over The fire till The anchoves be disolved put in a glass of red wine, mix the Butter with sume grated nuttmeg & a little flower.

Sause for Beef Stake's

Take Butter & fry it in a pan with some bits of beefe 'till looks brown ; then Take some gravey of lean Beefe, a little onion & some whole peper a few sweet herbs & fry it together, Then Take the flower box & shake some flower in it mix it well together & Strain it off & make it hott & pour it on The stakes when There are broiled.

An Excellent Syllabub

Tak sack or white or Red wine & some Cream & some suger put in Together & let stand two hours Then milk it full from The cow.

Boiled Plum, Pudding

Take a pound of beefe suett finely sheard half a pound of Raisons Stoned & Shread fine 4 good Spoonfull of fine flower four spoonfull of suger 5 eggs a little Slat[29] & nuttmeg, mix all These well together The longer it boils The Better it is.

Lemon Puff's

Take a pound of flower, half a pound of Butter or rather less one large or two samll Lemons Cut off The peal & Sheard it very fine Then Take out the sead & beat the pulp all to mash, Then Take a little cinnamond or mace beaten fine mix all These well in The flower & sweeten it to your Tast before you put The Butter in ; make it a Stiff past with water Then roal it out but not to Thin & cut Them into what shapes you please fry Them in Butter, sift some suger over Them Garnich The Dish with Lemon.

Rice Cheese Cakes

Take four ounces of flower of Rice boil it in a quart of milk or Cream 'till Thick Then Stur in Three quarters of a pound of fresh Butter & Eggs leave out half The whites, a little Beaten mace the rind of a lemon cutt very fine putt Them into Thin pufft past, a little Time will Bake Them (add some currents to Them).

Almond Cream's

A pound of Almonds beaten small & Strained out with Cream & boil Them in a quart of Cream with some orang flower water & suger & yolks of Eggs until it be as Thick as pap so servit, note you must be carefull in boeling it That it does not turn & be sure stir the Creem all one way & keep it stiring for some Time after it is of The fire.

A Hedghogg Puding

Take a quarter of a pound of Almonds blanchd reserve a 20 of Them to cut in Quarters The rest beate very fine with a little rose water beate five yolks & Three white with Three Spoonfulls of rose water about a pint of Cream Sweeten with suger & put in The beaten Almonds & Stire it well put in a penny lofe bening[30] grated and mix it very well togerther Then tye it up in napking & boyl it an houre Then Turn it in dish & Stick in all The other quarter of The Almond one The top of it round it, pour The Butter with rose water & suger upon it & secarce[31] suger one The top, & sarve it up.

To Make Little Puff

Take a good handfull of new milk Cheess Curd whayed very dry & beate it in a wooding bole very small, put in 4 Eggs & two whites a little Salt nuttmeg Simnomond & grated beard[32] as will make it all most as Stife as past beate it well together and make it up in to little flat cakes butter a paper and lay Them upon it and bake Them The oven must not be to hott when They look Brown They are enought a quarter of an hour will back Them serve them up at a second corse with Butter beaten with rose water & suger.

To Dry Neats Toungs Red

When They come new in lay Them six hours in pumpe water Then lay Them 12 days in stronge brine made with Spanish Salt & a little Salt peter & pumpe water that will Bear an Egge if you cannot get Spanish Salt whit & bay salt mixed will do your brine must not be boyled Then Take Them out & dry Them in a cloath & dry salt Them with Spanish salt & Salt peter or instead of Spanish salt, white salt and bag Salt with Slat[29] peter mixed so lett Them lye 14 days if They be stife before you may Take Them out & Dry Them in The chimney or oven which you pleaes.

To Make Eggs Pyes

Take about 30 Eggs & beat Them very well Then put Them into a broad dish or panne & sett Them on a hott fire as you doe to butter & keep them Stirring for fear they shoul burme you must make them as dry as very you can all in to little crumbles Then to a pound & half of These Eggs Take a pound & half of rason stoned & 16 dates Then sheard all These Together very fine with some 5 pounds of Sewet or some Thing beeter as you secoecasion Then season it with spice salt and a good dleale of orange & lemond peal, cut Extreame small & a goodle of Vinger & rose water & 4 good pipen's sheard There must be three pound of Currants, The reason must be stoned before you weight Them & you must sweeten Them to your Tast, you must put Vinger to all your mince pye's for it give Them a very fine Tast & lay dats Cittern and orange & marrow one The Tope.

To Make Lemon Jelly

Take Lemon pare Them Thin roal & beate Them 'till They are a little soft. Then roast Them in an apple roaster & when hott Throgh cut Them & squeese out The juce and strain it, Take The full weight in duble refine suger, sett it over The fire which must not be to hott keep it stiring Constantly & let is scald 'till it looks Clear, it will Jelly & keep a weeke . . .

To Bake a Leg of Beef

Take a Large Leg of Beef. Cut out all the Sinors from the Lean put them at the bottom of a pan, take a Onion, cut in too, stick it full of Cloves & put thereon with a Little Mace, Season it with Pepper & Salt as you like, then take the Lean & cut it in pieces & put over the Sinors & a Faggot of Sweet Herbs Season it as before, then brake the bones & Lay on the top of the Meat (Put no water in the Pan) tye it over with a sheet of Brown paper, Sent[33] it to the Oven overnight to put in with the Bread till next day Dinner, & when comes home take off the Bones & Lean meat & Scum off the fatt

24

then take out the Sinors & Gravy. Put it in a small Soup Dish with Toasted bread in Squars or otherwise Garnish & sarve it up to Table.

Mrs Bolly Lambert Way to Make an October Orange Pudding[34] 1760

Take the Peel of 3 or 4 Sevil oranges and Pare off the Rind as far as they are yellow then boil the Bitterness Pretty well out shifting the water 2 or 3 times then Blanch and beat a quarter of Pound of almonds very Fine a Pound of Loaf suger and 3 quarters of a Pound of Fresh butter the yolks of 16 eggs and 3 Naple Biskets Grated but this all together in a stone morter till it be all of one colour Past the Dish Put in the Pudding and Past it over But the Peel first by it self and the almonds by them selves and then beat them both to gether and Put in the Bisket the Last thing.

To Make a Costard for Ditto

Take a quart of cream Boil it with a stick of Cinnamon and a Lorrel Life[35] in it sit it to cole[36] the yolks of 8 eggs will beaten suger to yor tast when cold Put yor cream to yor eggs and strain them all to gever then fil yor cups for Baking they must be but just hard if milk then 12 eggs.

To Make Everlasting Syllibubs for Ditto

Take a quart and half a Pint of crame a Pint of Rhinish $\frac{1}{2}$ a Pint of sack 3 Lemons near a Pound of Doubble refine suger Beat and souft the suger and Put it in to your crame Grate if[37] the yellow rind of your 3 Lemons and Put that in squees the Juice of the 3 Lemons into your wine and Put that to yor crame then Beat all to gether with a which[38] just half an hour then take it uup all to gether with a spoon and fill your Glases it will keep good for 10 days and is best 3 or 4 days old.

4$^{oz.}$ white sugar Candy beat to Powder
4$^{oz.}$ of Iar Raisin's, stoned & shred
4$^{oz.}$ of Conserve of Roses
4$^{oz.}$ of the Hardest Apples Pared & Cored

40. Drops of Vitriol
40. Drops of Sulphur (not Balsom)

All beat up in a Stone Mortar, when made, Eats like a preserved Sweatmeat, is as fine as the puff of a Roasted Apple & is as Red as a Cherry, is a fine thing for a Cough, Hoarseness, Consumption, Hooping Cough, Asthma & Paralytick Disorders, you may take a Teaspoonfull, or Two, any time of the Day, when you cough or going to Bed, or Morning, you may Eat, Drink, & go abroad as usual. I have Experienced it among my Own Friends in surprising Manner, & among Persons of Quality who respect me for it

London April 2^d. 1760. Recommended by S^r. y^r Homble

Servt

John Waters

If your Family makes it up it will cost at 18 or 19³⁹ if made up by an Apotherary it will cost 2/6. but don't let the Apotherary know what it is good for.

PART TWO

Part Two

From Sister Mason

Stakes of a Line of Mutton

Cutt it in to slices & season it wth as much nutmegg pepper
and salt as w^{ll} ly upon a shilling y^n take 2 or 3 spoonfulls of
Capers onyons a little and mince y^m together & add to it
half a pint of oysters 3 anchovis & a quarter of a pint of
white wine & half a slyced Lemon y^n fry it all together till it
be tender y^n beat 3 Eggs & 2 spoonfulls of virjuce & put in
ye pan a good peic of butter & dish it take ye stakes of a Loyne
or neck of mutton or veale & seson it wth ye same ingredients
as you did ye former Lyne & stewe it in a pipkin wth half a pin
of water and half a pint of white whine y^n dish it wth sippits
pit[40] in a good pice of butter.

To Souce an Elle[41]

Scource the Elle wth a handfull of salt then splitt it down the
back and take out the chine bone & season it wth nutmegg
pepper and salt and minced sweet herbs then roal it up like
a coler of Brawn and tye a thred ateach end and in the middle
then boyle it in water and salt and vineger & six bleads of
mace and sliced lemon then boyl it an hour and keep it in
ye same liquor two or thre days then cut it out in roud
pices[42] & lay 6 or 7 in a dish wth thyme and parsley and
saucers of vineger ye same Ingerdients w^{ll} serve a pigg Capon
Calves feet or Legg of mutton or Calves head only add half
a pint of white wine in the liquor and Jelly or shreed
Cucumbers in the saucers.

From Ann Bruton

To Stew a Rabit or a Hear

Quarter him and wash him and of nutmeg Cloves Mace
Cinaman & pepper of each a small quantity & mix it wth

salt y^n take a small quantity of pot time and marjorum &
strip & shed y^m mix ye spice and herbs toogether and so
season ye rabit wth it there must be a small quntity of water
in ye stewing as mich as will cover ye botom of ye pot or
something more it must stew gently for an hour and a half
& before you take it off ye fire you must put in a good peice
of buttor & shake it about if you stew a Hear 2 or 3 hours
it w^{ll} be little enough.

To Make
Beef Pudding

Take a pound of Beef & as much Suet & mix it as for mince
peyes take of nutmeg cloves mace peper and salt of each of
all these as much as w^{ll} season it to make it savoury meat
take also a small quantity of sweet marjorum & broad time
shred very small together y^n put it into ye rest of ye seasoning
take half a pound of Currents well washed and mix wth y^e
meat when all these things are well mixed together take two
egs and 5 or 6 spoonfulls of Sack & 4 of Vineger beat ye sack
& vineger wth ye egs & put it in to ye meat then make as
much pufpast as will rowll it up in too patts to boyl 2 hours
w^{ll} boyl y^m.

To Coller
a Brest of Veal

Take a brest of veal bone him and season him wth peper
Cloves mase & salt as much as w^{ll} make savoury meat take
also some bread thime a small Quantity of sweet marjorum
shed ye herbs & mix wth ye seasoning when you have mixt it
all together then strow it all over ye inside of ye Veal y^{en}
lay some thin slices of bacon upon ye seasoning bate 3 Eggs
wth 3 sponfulls of vineger & put it all over on ye seasoned side
of ye Veal then roul it up in ye Caul & fillit it round wth
tape it w^{ll} ask 2 or 3 hours roasting when it is done take of y^e
fillit & Cut it in 2 in ye middle and set ye Collers upright in
ye dish you may make sauce wth buttor Vineger & mustard
it w^{ll} eat very well Cold.

From Esqure Sands of Miserdine[43]

To Make Oringe or Lemon Cadle[44]

Take a pint of water one large Oring or Lemon pear off y^e
pill[45] & put it in to ye Wate letting it stand all night in y^e
morning squise ye Juse take ye yolks of 4 Eggs & ye white of
2 beat y^m very well puting y^m in y^e water wth a little suger
when it is very well boylt sweten it to your taste if you have
not time to steep your pill[45] you may boy it, it is best cold.

From Mary Hill

To Pickle Kidny Beans

You must take those y^t are very young and tender when they
are very small gather them in a day y$^{t's}$ dry then they must
be scalded & boyl very gently in a skillit of fair water tell
they are very tender but not break when they are done take
them up in a cullender draining y^m well from y^e water sett
y^m by to coole then take a quart of vineger or more or less
according to the quantity of beans then take of Cloves Mase
hole pepper wth 2 or 3 Races of ginger so much of these
spices as w^{ll} make ye pickle tast prety strong of it you must
also boyle soe much salt as w^{ll} make it tast prety sharp of it
a pice of Oring or Lemon pell[45] w. doe very well to boyl wth
ye spices in it when it is done take it off & set it by to cole y^e
next morning put ye beans in ye pickle they must be put in a
deep narrow pot ye pickle must cover them ty y^m down wth
a lether when ye pickle grows mouldey & decays boyl y^m up
again and put the beans in.

To Make a Little Plum Cake

Take 2 pound of flower one pound of Currents take half a
pint of Ale yest and first lay a leven in your flower season it
wth spice seeds suger salt & Rose water to your taste put in
3 eggs then boyl a pint of cream & slise 3 quarter of a pound
of of butter into a pan then power your Cream on it when it is
a little more then blood warm & ye leven ris temper ye Cake
3 Quarters of an houre w^{ll} bake it butter your pan or hoop

it is baked in if you would have sweet meats or Allmonds there w[ll] want more Yest.

To Make a Karrat Pudding

Take a quart of Cream & half a pint of Milk & 7 eggs keep out 3 of y[e] Whites take 3 or 4 karrats clensed & washed & great y[m] then take the quantity of half a peney loaf greated also mix all this together in a pan & stur it well put in suger salt & Nutmeg to your taste when it goes into y[e] Oven you must melt almost a quarter of a Pound of fresh buttur & stur it in y[e] pudding you may put in sweetmeats a Canded Oring Lemons & sitten pills[46] morry[47] w[ll] do very well to stick on y[e] Pudding when it goes into y[e] Oven you may take y[e] 3 Whites y[t] you keept out of y[e] Pudding & make a thin puf paste wth a little Sugar in it to line y[e] dish you bake it in you must put in y[e] Buttor & sweetmeats just as it goes in y[e] Oven & stur it or esce y[e] sweetmeats w[ll] sink to y[e] bottom one hour w[ll] beak y[m].

From Sister Mason

To Bottle Goosberys for Tarts

Take y[e] largest Goosberys when they are att the full growth before they turn to be ripe & pick off the stocks & heads and have your bottle fitted wth Corcks so tite y[t] they w[ll] hold water lett y[m] be well drained & dried for if either Goosberys or bottle be wet it w[ll] spoyl them fill them full & Corck them tie & sett them up to y[e] neck in water in a Copper and lay a weight on y[e] top of each bottle for to keep y[m] steddy let y[m] stand in scalding but not to boyl about 6 or 8 hours I sett y[m] in att 6 or 7 a clock at night and lett them stand till they are cold for they are to stand in that water all nighth till they are cold.

From Mary Hill

To Make a Little Cake

Take a pound of flower 1 Pound of Currents take haf a pint of Ale yest & first lay a Leven in your flower season it w[th]

spice seeds sugar salt & Rose water to your taste put in 3
eggs then boyl a pint of cream & slice 3 quarters of a pound
of butter into a pan then power your cream to it when it is
a little warmer y^n blood & ye leaven ris temper ye Cake 3
quarters of an hour w^{ll} bake ye Cake butter your pan or
hoop it is bak'd in if you would have sweetmeats and
Allmonds it w^{ll} require more yest.

To Make Pudding of Calves Feet

Take 2 Calves feet boyl them 3 howers then [48] them but
before they are quite cold mince them as small as for pyes
put as much beef suet minced as w^{ll} make them fit for pyes
season it wth mace nutmeg salt & sugar to your taste then put
4 spoonfulls of each put all these ingedients together in a
pan & mix them well togather wth as much cream as w^{ll}
make a tender pudding 3 howers w^{ll} boyl it it must be boyld
in a beson or pudding pot well buttered you must put in
Currents as you like it many or few.

From Hanah Fream

To Make Jemeca Trouts or Pickled Herrings

Take ye herrings take out ye Gutss & take out ye rows &
scale y^m lay y^m 1 laying on another salted in a pan 24 hours
then take y^m out & wipe y^m dry then put y^m in a pan fit to
bake y^m in lay a laying of fish & little Gemeca pepper hool[49]
between each laying then fill up the pot wth ye best wine
vinager then bake it 6 howers when it is coold take off ye fat
they are then fit to eat & w^{ll} keep good in their pickle a
quarter of year you may eat them wth Oyl Vineger lemmon
or pepper. Tie a shet of brown pape over ye pan when it
goes into ye Oven.

To Make a Cake

Take 3 quarters of a peck of fine flower & 3 pints of yest 6
Eggs 6 pound and a half of Butter 1 Pound of Cettron 1
pound of sugar 2 Ounces of Carraway seeds half a pint of
sack a Little saffron one ounce of Nutmeggs half an ounce

of Cloves & mace & sinnamon a Race or 2 of Ginger beaten 10 pounds of Currents wet it wth cream or Milk make it Limber & lett it stand by ye fire a Riseing tell it goes into ye Oven. To Ise ye Cake take 4 pound of Double Refind sugar 4 Whites of Eggs a Little Rose Water & beat them well together and put it on when it comes out of ye Oven.

To Make Damson Wine

Fill a Vessell allmost full wth Damsons then fill it wth good clear water well boyld let it sand^{50} 24 howers skim it clean & put to Every Gallon ½lb of ye best sugar stering it a while to make it desolve after put it up in a vessell & when it has done working stop it up & Keep it 3 Months or it may be keept 2 Years.

From Hanah Norton

To Pot Beef Venason or Hare

Take ye under lift of ye Buttock of beef cut it into little pices & take off all ye skin & fatt season it pretty well wth salt Jemeca pepper & other pepper lay it in a pot a laying of beef & a laying of suet minc'd fine betwen every laying half a pint of white wine a bundle of sweet herbs paste ye pot close and put it in ye oven all night when it is quite coold take out ye meat & dry it wth a cloth and mince it as fine a possable. if it wants seasoning you may add more then put it in ye pan you keep it in, & press it close wth your hand & lay butter all over it put it in ye Oven again about a quarter of an hower when it is coold press it close wth your hand & cover it over wth cllarefied butter.

To Pickle Artichoaks

Cutt ye leaves to ye choacks thin throw ye bottom choak and all into y^e water or they w^{ll} turn black when they are all so prepar'd throw them into a kettle of boyling water lett them boyl a little till you can pull y^e choak verry hardly from them then throw itt into could water again firstt pulling off

all y^e choak then into saltt water thatt w^ll bare an Egg wth a quartt of vineager and cover them wth Oyl.

To Make a Carraway Cake

Tak 3 pound of fine flower & dry it over a Cafing dish[51] of Coals y^n take 3 qurs. of a pound of suger & put to it 2 ounces of Caraway seds when these are mix'd together take half a pint of Ale yest a quarter of a pint of Rosewater 3 Eggs make a leven of this & let it lay a little while to rise boyl $\frac{1}{2}$ a pint of Crear[52] & boyl it and when it is a little more y^n blood warm slice in $\frac{1}{2}$ a pound of Buttur and mix y^e Cake very tender & put it in a pan y^t may be fitt for it & take heed y^t y^e Oven be not to hot 1 houre w^ll bake it.

To Make Fine Biscakes

Brake 4 new laid Eggs Take one White & a half out & all y^e treds clean from them beat them wth 4 soonfulls of rose water & 4 spoonfulls of fair Water & 1 pound o Dob. Refin'd Lo. sug^r. beaten and sersed beat all these together 1 hower & a $\frac{1}{4}$ while y^e Oven is heating wch must be as hott as for white bread when you swep y^e Oven the Oven stir in a pound all but 2 Ounces of y^e finest flower well dired[53] put in Coriander seeds well dried to your own liking bake them in Little tinn pans fill them not to full.

From Sister Mason

To Candy Angellicoe

Take green & young Angellicoe & Cutt off ye Leaves then put it in a Kettle wth some water & Cover it wth the Leaves & then set it over y^e fire & Lett it boyl untill it is tender then take it up & peel off y^e Upper skins then sett on y^e water again and lett it just boyl then dip y^e Angellicoe in then take it up & sett it then dry it in a Cloath then take it and weigh it and take $\frac{3}{4}$^lb of single refin'd sugar beaten & serced very fine to a pound of Angellicoe then lay y^e Angelligo in rows in an earthen pan & strow a handfull of sugar betwen every row then let it stand untill all y^e sugar is desolv'd then

set it over a Clear Chorcoal fire & let boyl & stirr it sometimes till ye sugar is almost boyld away then take it up &
twist it & put it Upon thin pleats till it is dry.

To Pott Carp or Troutt

Take your Carp scale and draw them slitt yhem in three or
four places to the bone and season them wth Cloves Mace and
Nutmegs and peper beatt ye spice small and putt as much
saltt as you think fitt than bake them in a pott laying a good
deall of butter upon them and under y^m covering them verry
close and lett them sand[50] in a hott Oven four hours draw
them and putt them into a pott presing them wth a spoon
and cover y^m wth ye clear of butter they were baked in, nextt
day meltt more butter and fill ye Pott.

A Receipt
to Make Pig Brawn

Take a large sow pigg well fed & 6 weeks old or upward ;
when it is scalded & drest cut off the head closs to ye shoulders
cut off ye feet as you doe when yee roast one, y^n cutt down
clean through ye Chine in ye back y^n bone it leaving as little
flesh as you can upon ye bones lay ye bones by all together for
use as heareafter y^n cut ye 2 sides of ye pig in halves for 4
collars lay it in a Cloth to dry & get these harbes & spices
to season it wth, (viz) Thyme sweet marjorum Winter savory
Parsly sorrol & a little tender sage wch must be stript &
shread small as to be like ye spices beat ye spices as Nutmegs
Cloves Mace & a few corns of peper shred in, Mix all these
together according as it w^{ll} answer your tast, also to it y^n
strow ye herbes & spice in ye midst of ye quarters rubing it
into y^m rowl y^m up for Collers (keeping y^t for ye out side w^{ch}
was cut through in ye middle because it is evinest y^n sew
y^m wth big white thread draw it through a little white wax
y^n sew y^m close in thin Holland baggs put ye same seasoning
into ye ears mouth & neck of ye Pigs head sewing it up allso
in a thin fine cloth. Whilst your collers are thus geting ready,
let your liquor be set onn wch must be thus, set onn a Skillet
rather deeper y^n broad put into it 3 Quarts or a Gallong one

quart of white wine one Pint of Vineger A good spoonfull of whole peper & salt enough to season it pretty well but not to salt because it is to be boyld to a Jelly afterwards put 3 Slic'd Nutmeg Cloves & Mace according as ye like it put allso a hansom bundle of herbs as Thym, Winter-Savory & sweet Marjorum put in also ye bones bol it & scum it & when ye bones are enough boild take them out & put in the head & collars & boy y^m till tender then take them out & put up in some flat dish or platter y^n boyl ye Liquor about at quarter of an houre after y^t is out y^n take out ye bundle of hearbs & power it into some earthen pot Nex morning take off ye cases from ye Collars & head & put y^m into an earthen Vessel y^t ye intend to keep y^m in standing up an end[54] & ye head in ye middle. If ye Liquor be jellied then set it on & warm it till it be disolved & pour it upon ye collars so as to cover y^m if it be not jellied it must be boyld again & when cold pourd on as before.

These large piggs their heart liver & inwards w^{ll} make a very fine Pudding thus ordred parboil ye Liver break it in a Mortar wth yolks of eggs, a few spoonfulls of cream some spice & a little salt & work it so together y^n put it into some shred savory herbs as before in ye pigg brawn & beef suet.

To Make
RICE PUDDING

Take a pound of rice pick it and wash it boyl it a little in water or scim milk till it be well plumpt y^n put it in a cullender or a Sive to drain it from ye liquor y^n boyl it in about 3 pints of 2 quarts of milk when it is tender enough take it off stive it up close in ye pot or pan & before it is too could uncover.

To Make
CHICKIN PIE IN WINTER

Take ye Chickin and cut y^m in peises then Season y^m wth Cloves & Mace & Nutmeg sugar & salt dried Cheries Candid oringe Lemon & Sittern ye yolks of 4 or 5 hard Egs & butter and a little water.

A Cordiall to Put Into it

Take ye yolks of 3 eggs & white wine heat it verry hot then work it togather wth sugar & Butter if ye pey be not fat enough.

To Make Chickin Pie in ye Summer

Cut them in pices y^n season y^m wth Cloves & mace & Nuttmegg Salt Sugar Green-Pease ye bottom of Hartichoaks Cherries Goosbereys & Yolks of 4 Hard Eggs.

To Stew Ducks or Geese

Boil them in water with Jemeka Pepper Onyons white peper & Salt.

To Stew Cabbidges

Take ye Cabidges & half boil y^m then take y^m out & not cruch them so put them into ye Stew Pan and Jamaka Pepper & a little mace pounded, put in tow or 3 bay Leaves when half Stewd put in some Creame & 2 Anchovis when you take it up stir in some Butter.

For Fish Sauce

Take ye pickle of ye Fish Clarret Anchovis a little lean Bacon a Little Lemon pill & Cowcumbers & Butter.

A Sauce to Boild Chickin

Take Spinage & Sorrel pound them togather & press out ye Juse y^n take Vineager & Sugar scalde some Gooseberries or grapes in sugar & water tost some white Bread & Cut it into Sippets & lay y^m round ye dish then heat ye Sauce & put in some Butter y^n put ye goos berrys in ye dish when your Sauce is in.

To Stew Carps

Souce y^m wth Salt till all ye Scaales be off y^n dry them Cut y^m behind ye head to make y^m bleed and save the bloud y^n take a Bottle of Sider & Clarret Stick a Oynion full of Cloves &

put it into it y^n put in half a pint of Water put in ginger & Mace Pepper & Sinamon Horse Radish & Anchovis boil y^m togather before the Carp go in; Stew them about half an houre then turn y^m Put in a Crust of white bread ye yolks of 3 Eggs; y^n take ye bloud & mingle y^m all togather wth ye Spaune so shake it up wth butter.

To Mumble a Rabet

Boil ye Rabet half y^n take it & Cut it in pices y^n take a Bunddle of sweet herbs a Onion or 2 Anchovis boil 2 or 3 Eggs hard & Chop y^m verry small y^n take out ye herbs & shake it up wth Butter.

Wild Duck Sause

Clarit, Anchovis, & the Liver Boyld & crusht through a Sife, Soe Shake it up wth Butter.

To Collar Beef

Take a thin pice of ye brest and bone it, then Rub it wth salt Peeter & let it lie 12 Hours y^n soak it in pump water make your water salt wth Common Salt before you put in your beef, let it lie in water 3 or 4 days then take a pretty bigg Nutmeg & Cloves & mace proportionable to it then mince 7 bay leaves verry small y^n roul it up verry hard wth Incle puting it into a high pot then cover it wth ye Pickle, and bake it wth a batch of bread.

A Friggise of
Chickins or Rabits

Cut them in peeces then fry it in butter then make some Strong broth, put in Cloves, Mace, Nutmegs, Mushromes, pickled Oysters, Lemon peel, Onyons, a little Cowcomber, & Claritt thicken it wth Cream, Flower, & the Yolks of 4 Eges, then Shake it up wth Butter.

Doe Veal or Capones the Same way only put in more Onyons.

To Stew a Rump of Beefe

Stufe it wth Sorill, Spinig, time, Margerum, pursly, Onyons, a little Lemon Peele, Jemaica pepper pounded very small alittle Mace & Beefe Suit, you must Stufe it very well, put in as much Water as will allmost cover it; pit in pickled Pursland, Cowcumbers 4 or 5 Bottles of Sidar 5 or 6 Bay leaves, a little whit peppar & Salt, Cover it downe very close & Stew it wth a gentle Fire.

To Make Plume Pottage

Take a Leg of Beefe & Shine & boyle them all to peeces then Straine ye meat out of the broth, then boyle a Crust of Bread in ye Broth, put in Cloves, Mace, Nutmegs, Reasons of ye Sun, Sinoment a good deale pruans, Currants, Sake & Clarratt Sweetening it wth Sugar, thicken it wth grated whit bread.

To Make Capon Sause

Small bear, & a little Floure in it, Clarrit, Ancovis pickled Cowcombers ye livers boyled & crushed through a Sive Soe Shake it up wth Butter.

To Make Elder Wine From Ditto

Take 1 Gallon of spring water boil it & when it is allmost could poure it upon 5^lb of malagas Pict rub'd & Chop't & let it stand 4 Days stiring it twise a Day then Draw it off having in rediness so much of ye Juse of Elder berrys as will colour it of a Claret Couler mix it together & let it stand a quarter of a Year before it is taped.

To Dry Apricocks

Take ye Apricocks stone & Pear y^m take a little above halfe their weight in Double refin'd sugar finely beaten & as you stone & pare y^m fill ye holes & roule y^m in sugar when that's done poure ye rest of ye sugar upon them & let y^m stand 7 or 8 houres then boil them gently till they look clear & let them stand in ye surrop 2 days y^n scald or boyl y^m a little ye next day & lay y^m on a hair sive to Draine y^n sift a little fine sugar on y^m & set y^m to drie in a stew.

To Pickle French Beanes

Take a ligar[55] make it strong enough wth salt to bear an egg y^n put in your French beans & lett y^m lie in untill they grow verry yellow wch w^{ll} be a week or 9 days y^n take y^m out & put y^m in cold water & hang y^m over ye fire & keep y^m scalding & poure cold water upon y^m 5 or 6 times as they are dooing till they are green, when green enough let y^m boil till tender y^n take y^m out of ye water & lay y^m upon a board to coole y^n make your pickle wch must be of white wine vineegar & little pepper & ginger & put in salt enough to bare an egg y^n boil it when it boils take it off ye Fire & put it in a pan when its cold & your beans cold put in yor beans & ty y^m up fast.

To Pickle Mangoe

Take learge Coucumbers open y^m wth a Narrow mouth'd spoon & take out all ye Jucy part Clean y^n put in a little Mustard a little clove of Garlick & a little Jamace Pepper into each Coucumber & y^n close y^m togather & tie y^m wth a thread, Then make your Pickle wch must be White wine Vinegar strong enough to bare an egg wth salt a little ginger & a little Jamace peper boil your pickle & poure it on 2 or 3 times as you do your Coucumber if not green enough put y^m over ye Fire in ye Pickle.

To Pickle Coucumbers

Take yor coucumbers lay y^m in salt & water 2 Hours wash y^m out & let y^m draine cut some fennill & dill stalks Jamace Pepper & Ginger some fennill & dill seeds Lay some of ye Stalks & strew some of ye seeds & spice in ye bottom of a rundle fit for yor Coucumb^{rs} y^n put in some Coucumb^{rs} & about ye middle put some more stalks & seeds & spice, fill up ye vessel wth Coucumb^{rs} lay some more spice seeds & stalks on ye top, & have it headed up close boil yor vinegar seasoned wth salt & a little of ye spice poure it scalding hot to yor Coucumb^{rs} & sop y^m close & about a week after scald y^m again.

To Pickle Coucumbers

Take ye small sort of Pickling Coucumbers lay y^m in an earthen pan & make yor water as salt as for small Brine boil it up scum it & power it on ye Coucumbers scalding hot y^n cover it close and wrap it round wth wollen cloaths to keep in ye breath let it stand 4 or 5 Days make your pickle of ye best wine vinegar spice according to youer quantity wch is cloves mace white Pepper Jamaco pepper & 2 Nutmegs quartered boyl in a little Dill keep of yor spice to strow betwixt ye laying of yor Coucumbers y^n take yor Coucumbers from ye water & lay y^m on Cloths to dry y^n put y^m in yor pickling pot strowing in ye spice between y^n power on yor pickle boiling hot, they should be keept in stone pickling Jars fil'd well wth corks.

If yor coucumbers do not look well boyl them a little in ye pickle & put y^m all in hott again & stop y^m close.

To Pickle French Beans

Take y^m small & putt y^m in water & salt so strong as to bear an egg lett them lay 7 or 8 days lay a little board on to keep y^m under water y^n make a pickle of ye best wine vinegar of cloves mace & Jamaco pepper according to your quantity y^n dry youre beans from ye water & salt y^n put y^m in a brass kettle wth your vinegar & spice boyl y^m a little y^n take y^m off & put y^m in yor pickling pots wth pickle & all wth a bitt of allum stop y^m down close wth corks while they are hott take y^m at ye beginning of ye season they w^{ll} y^n be greenest.

Scotch Collops

Take Veal & cut it thine pieces then take some sweet herbs minse them very small wth Cloves Mace & Nutmegs pounded wth a little salt then put it on your Veale Fry it in Butter, make some strong broath, put in Mushromes, Anchovis & Clarrit & pickled Oysters & butter make veal bales & Frey them broune, take ye Yolks of 2 or 3 Eges then dip ye Clary in it, then Frye it Broune then slise some Baken thin & Fry it, then lay it on your Meat.

To Mark French Bread

Take half a bushel of fine flower on ye over night set a leaven wth 5 spoonfulls of water & 2 or 3 of yest mix it wth ye flower and lett it stand till ye next morning then take a Quart of Ale yest ye white of 25 Eggs beat y^m till they have done bubling y^n take 2 Quarts of new milk a Quart or more of water both boil'd togather & when it is scalding hot mix it togather wth ye flower make it verry soft & knead it but verry little but mould it togather till it Blisters Then let it lie a little & y^n mould it into little loaves & put it into wodden dishes y^n let it stand till it rises and craks on ye topp then put it into a quick Oven & lett it stand stop'd a houer y^n take it out & Rasp it as you use it; If they grow tough then put it into a warm oven a day or 2 after.

To Collar a Pigg

A Calves Foot Pudding

Take 2 Calves feet mince y^m well and as much beef suit minc'd grated bread as either ye like quantity of crrans[56] 2 eggs 1 white season wth nutmeggs cloves mace a little salt & sugar to yor taste 3 spoonfulls of rose water & as much cream as w^{ll} as w^{ll} make it of a sufficient thikness for a bagg Pudding lapp it up in ye Caule of a Lamb tying it long ways y^n put it up in a Cloth to boyl in water one hower serve it up wth freach butter sack & sugar for sauce.

To Make Curran Clear Cakes   Mary Emery

Take half a pound of Lofe Suger ye like waight ye juse of curans but ye Suger must be ye begger [57]waight put youer Suger into a Skilet wth noe more water y^n to wett it Scum it boyle it to a candy haight y^n put in ye juce boyle & scum it till it be a very stif jely redy to candy y^n power it into litle glases or dishes smoth at Botum fit to turn out & dry of ye thicknes of thin cakes if they are right they will be canded without

43

and moist within it must be 4 or 5 days befor you turn them out on glas to dry in a coold ovin or worme harth & in ye sun by degres.

To Make an Orange Puding   Cosien Fallconer

Take a quarter of a pound of fish. buter ye same of sugar ye youlkes of 8 Eggs beat all together in a stone mortor y^n take ye outward rinde of a larg & good cavil oring[58] wth ye ingredience aforesaid beat it well in ye mater[59] till all be well incopoted[60] wth a litle of ye juce of ye oring put it in a dish between too shets of pufpast, & bake it in an ovin heated all most as hot as for mainchet.

To Make Damson Wine

Fill a vessell almost full with Damsons, then fill it up with good cleen water well boyled, Let it stand 24 houres y^n draw it out & let it stand in an open Vesell 24 hours Skimm it clean & put to evrey gallon $\frac{1}{2}$^{lb} of C. Sugar stering it a while to make it disolve after put it up in a Vessell & when it has done working, stopp up y^e vessell & keep it three monthes or it may bee kept two years.

To Dry Apricocks

Take the Apricocks stone & Paire them y^n take a litle above halfe thare waght of Duble refined sugar finely beaten & as you stone & Paire them fill the holes & roule them in sugar when thats dune Poure ye rest of ye sugar upon them & let them stan 7 or 8 hours y^n boyle y^m Gentely till they loke Clear & let y^m stand in ye surop 2 days y^n scald or boyle y^m a letle ye next day & lay y^m one a hair Sive to Drain after wch sift a litle fine sugar upon them so set y^m in a stow to dry.

To Make Past of Quinces A F Iun^r.

Take your clearest Quinces & those that are freest from Specks let them boyle very fast til they are tender, pare y^m & drive ye Pulp through an hayr Sive, take to every pound of pulp a pund of Sugar, candy your Sugar & when it is at a

Candie height, y^n stir in your Pulp & mix it over a fire, till it is throughly mixt then take it of & put it into your plates you neede not let it boyle you must keepe your pulp on a Chafingdish of coales, till your Suger is candied.

Dr Feildings Way
to Make Meth

Take of Rosa Solis Virga Aurea & Herb Robert according to Discression of Ground Ive two handfulls and as much harts tongue as you please boyl them in Seaven Eightt or 9 Gallallons of water till one is consum'd then take outt ye hearbs and putt in 5 Gallons of water and one Gallon of Honey an so proportionable till as much as ye honey is boyld away strain itt and Sett itt a working like Ale and when it is stopd up hang in ye vessell of Nutmeg mace Cinnamon and ginger of each 1 ounce itt may be drunk sooner if ye juse of a Lemmon or 2 Be putt in.

To Make Rattefea

Take four hundred of Apricock Stones and wipe them clean then bruse them in a coarss cloth and putt to them a gill of ye bestt french brandy wth one pound of double refind Sugar half an ounce of Cloves and Sinamon and 3 large Nuttmegs slic'd putt all these things togather into a large bottle wth half a drham of Cochaneall and shake itt well every morning for a month togather then filter itt wth filtring paper and twill be fitt for drinking butt lett itt be putt into glass bottles.

To Make
an Oring Puding   M C

Pear one larg Cheny Oring[61] uery thinn then beat the peell with sum of its oun Juse in a marble morter then take a pound of fresh butter and one pound of whit suger work the suger and butter togather then take 7 yolks and 3 whits of Eggs with the aboue said peel and the remaining Juse with sum Rose water and Sack to your tast all, which mix well togather line the dish you bak it in with Right fine pufpast it will want but half an hours baking or les.

To Make Past of Oringes
Mary Bellers

Take y[e] best Civile Oringes[62] clear & Sound & deepest colour scrape of all y[e] out side or Pare them very thin leaving y[e] Yellow, cut them in Halfs wring out y[e] juce & pick out y[e] clear meat & Save it in a pot clos covered but presently pick out all y[e] Seeds & Strings out of it for y[e] seeds standing in it will make it bitter lay y[e] Peels in fear[63] water 24 hourers Shifting them with fresh Water twise or thrise in y[e] time then boyle them in a good deale of Water close covered till they be very tender then take them Up & take out y[e] meat & dry them in a cloth then slice one half of them on a trencher very thin & beat y[e] other half in a Morter very fine take their weight in double refined Suger wett it in water in little lumps lump by lump & put in a very little of y[e] Water Set it over y[e] fier boyle it tell it draw high in y[e] mean time put all y[e] Peels together & put y[e] Juce to it, put it into another Skillit set it on y[e] fire & make it scalding hott when y[e] Suger is at y[e] height put in y[e] pulp keep it stiring all y[e] time & when it hase boyled sume time put it in glases for use.

To Pickle Neats Toungues

Take 1 handfull of common salt & 2 ounces of salt peter beat fine & a Quarter of a pound of coarse sugar & mingle all those together & rub y[e] tongues very well wth it put y[m] into an earthen pot this quantity will do y[e] Second time Boyl y[e] tongues without drying.

To Pickle Pork
Susannah Turner

Take y[e] belly peices of y[e] hogg & Cutt y[m] into such peices bigger or Lesser as you think fitt then Let y[m] Lye to drain from y[e] blood 24 hours y[n] rubb y[m] wth peter & bay salt very well Leaving it pretty thick on y[e] pork y[n] put it close into a pot Laying a bed of white salt at y[e] bott[m] of y[e] pot first & stop y[e] Cracks full with it betwixt y[e] meat thick Layed over y[e] top so y[t] y[e] meat may not touch one another nor y[e] pot no way nor any air get into ye meat or pot ye meat must be boned before it is salted.

To Make Rasbery Cakes

Put ye Rasberrys into a preserving pan & warm them gently over a few coles keeping them gently sturring from ye bottom & when The Liquor is pretty well come from them then put it into a boulter bag & let ye Liquor run from ye Rasburys & then way them & to every pound of them thus order'd take one pound & quarter of Loaf suger finely beat put ye suger into ye preserving pan & desolve it with as Little watter as possoble and boil it untel it almost comes to suger again then put in ye Rasberrys sturing them well & scum them well three or four minnuts will boyle them enough then drop them upon Earthen plates & put them in an oven that has very Little heat in it turning them every day upon fresh plats until dry.

A Receipt to Make Red Ink

Take two Ounces of Brazell, a Quart of fair Water & a dram of Allom half a Quarter of an Ounce of Gum Arraback then put your water in a Bellmettle skillet & let it boyle then put in your Brazell Allom & Gum & boyle it for a quarter of an hour & then strain it through a thick ragg & keep it for use.

Yours
Fettiplace Bellers.

To Pickle Mushrooms

Take ye buttons wash or peel them & boyle in a in a sufficient quantaty of milk & watter till thay grow tender (puting them in just when your Liquor begins to boyle) take them out & let them coole then put them into a pickle made with whitewine vineger Pepper & mace let them stand five or six days to drein from this Pickle then put them into another pickle made with white wine & whitewine vineger of each an equal part & a little spice, Thay keep best in a wide mouth'd goosbery bottle.

Mad Dog

DOCT^r MEAD'S REMEDY FOR THE BITE OF A MAD DOG.[64]

Let the Patient be blooded at the Arm 9 or 10 Ounces. Take of the Herb called in Latin Lichen cinereus Terrestris, in English, Ash-colour'd Ground Liverwort, clean'd dry'd and powder'd, half an Ounce.

Of black Pepper powder'd, two Drachms.

Mix these well togather, & divide the Powder into four Doses, one of which must be taken every Morning, fasting, for four Mornings successively, in half a Pint of Cow's Milk warm : After these four Doses are taken, the Patient must go into the Cold Bath, or a cold Spring or River, every Morning fasting, for a Month ; he must be dipt all over, but not stay in (with his Head above water) longer than half a Minute, if the Water be very cold : After this he must go in three times a Week for a Fortnight longer.

The Lichen is a very comon Herb and grows generally in sandy and barren Soils all over England. The right time to gather it is in the Months of October or November.

The Doct^r says in the Experience of above thirty Years, upon more than 500 Patients he has never known the above Remedy to fail of success : He says That the sooner the Medicine is taken after the Bite, the better, though he had often found it to answer, though not taken 'till a Fortnight, or even a longer time after it.

PART THREE

Part Three

Take 2 quarts of Soft water, boyl one ounce of pearl barly in it till it comes to a quart, then take ½ an ounce of Sperma Ceeti, and the yolkes of 2 New laid Eggs, beat these in a Murble Morter till they look like Cream ; take this out of the Morter & put in 2 ounces of Iourdan Almonds blanch'd beat them well, adding a little of the Barly water 'till the Almonds are small, then add more of the Barley water 'till it looks white like milk, strain this through a Cloth & pour the rest of the Barley water from the Barley into it, then add the Sperma Ceeti & yolks of Eggs, stirring all together put it into a Bottle Sweetning it with 2, 3 or 4 Ounces of Syrup of Balsam to your taste, then Shake it well for an hour & take four Spoonfulls Night & morning milk warm, Shaking the Bottle each time.

Take of

Gascoigns powder on Scruple
Russian Castor
Snake Root of Each 10 Grams
Oil of Amber one drop
Syrup of Saffron a Sufficient quantity to make all into a Bolus to be taken going to rest.

A Receipt

Take the best Rhubarb in Powder Two Ounces & half, Salt of Wormwood a Dram, Orange Peell half an Ounce, Grated Nutmeg Two Scruples, Cochineal half a Dram. Infuse Forty Eight Hours by a Warm Fire Side In a Quart of true Arrack, Strain it off & put it in a Well Cork'd Bottle for use.

An Excellent Remedy for a Cough

Take

Scorcinary Root .... 1. oz
Marsh Mallows Root .... 1. oz

51

White Cumphry Root . . . . 1. oz
Eringo Root, Candied . . . . 1. oz

Boil them in three pints of Spring Water to a Quart of which drink about half a pint every Morning in a little warm Milk.

P. E.

Reciept for the Tooth Acke

Take of Sp^t of Wine rectify'd ¼ ounce
Camphor 1 Dram
Opium 5 Grains
Chemical oil of Box 10 Drops
mix them for use.

A Receipt Against the Plague

Take of rue, sage, mint, rosemary, wormwood, & Lavinder, a handfull of each, infuse them togather in a Gallon of white wine Vinegar in a Stone pot close coured[65] upon warm wood ashes for four days or more, after which draw off the Liquor in to bottles & into every quart put N B (one receipt says an ounce to a quart) a quarter of an ounce of Camphire ; with this wash your mouth, rub your Loins, & temples every day, Snuf a little up your nostrill when you go in the air, & Cary about you some Spunge dipped in the same to smell to as ocation reqiuers.

The Notes

———

1   sem : probably for 'seam', the line which runs down the side of a fruit.
2   melted.
3   The last two figures of the date have either not been entered or have been washed out.
4   orange peel.
5   and stalked.
6   in.
7   dry.
8   pin.
9   thoroughly.
10   beer.
11   The spelling 'boy' for 'boil' is found six times and therefore seems to be deliberate. On the other hand, 'boyl' is the normal spelling.
12   thoroughly cold, or cooled.
13   almost cold.
14   presumably stands for 'yeast'.
15   Perhaps this word 'don', which occurs twice at the end of a recipe, is intended for 'done'.
16   reasonable, reasonably.
17   'is' omitted.
18   conceive. The writer of this section had a very clear hand but no idea of spelling.
19   candy.
20   one gallon.
21   kine.
22   one.
23   cinnamon.
24   bacon.
25   'you' omitted.
26   hours.
27   balm.
28   strain.
29   salt.
30   being.
31   searce.
32   bread.
33   set.
34   This and the following two recipes are written in a new hand, which is almost illegible. The writer seems unable to distinguish between B and P.

53

35 laurel leaf.
36 set it to cool.
37 off.
38 whisk.
39 about 18 or 19 pence.
40 put.
41 Eel.
42 round pieces.
43 Possibly from the village of Miserden, near Stroud, Gloucestershire.
44 'Cadle' is a form of the word 'caudle' (see glossary).
45 peel.
46 citron peel.
47 The reading is corrupt; possibly intended for 'murrey' (see glossary).
48 The word 'piccle' has been crossed out here, but nothing put in its place.
49 whole.
50 stand.
51 Chafing dish (see glossary).
52 cream.
53 dried.
54 on end.
55 liquor, i.e. water.
56 currants.
57 bigger.
58 Seville orange.
59 mortar.
60 incorporated?
61 China-orange, a sweet orange said to have been brought from China.
62 Seville oranges.
63 fair.
64 This extract from Dr Mead's works reads (unlike the rest of the manuscript) as though it had been copied from a printed text. In his *A Mechanical Account of Poisons in Several Essays*, London, 1702, Richard Mead (born Stepney, August 1673, died 16 February 1754) has a section on the mad dog, but this does not contain the remedy here quoted. Mrs Hannah Glasse quoted it in the first edition of *The Art of Cookery*, 1747. One may assume that Mead wrote it after 1702. The British Museum's copy of the 1702 edition has a manuscript copy of the *Remedy* pasted in at the front. It was printed in the collected edition of his works, *The Medical Works of Richard Mead*, vol. 1, London, 1762, pp. 89-90.
65 covered.

Glossary

———

ALLAWAY: this word is not in the dictionaries, nor have I traced it in the many books on horses published in the eighteenth century which I have consulted. It possibly stands for 'horse aloe' (originally used in veterinary medicine).

BELL-METAL: an alloy of 80 parts of copper and 20 of tin.

BOLUS: a soft round mass of anything medicinal to be swallowed at once, larger than an ordinary pill.

BOULTER-BAG: a bag used for sifting or straining.

BRAZIL: a heavy wood, red in colour, used in manufactures for dyeing red.

CADLE: see caudle.

CARDUS: probably *carduus benedictus*, or Blessed Thistle.

CAUDLE: a warm drink given to sick persons.

CAUL (of a lamb): a membrane investing the viscera.

CHAFING-DISH: a dish or vessel to hold coals for heating anything set on it; a portable grate for coals.

CHENEY: obsolete form of China.

COLLAR, to: to crop, pluck.

CUBEB: the small spicy berry of Cubeba officinalis from Java and the East Indies. It resembles a grain of pepper, but is somewhat larger, less aromatic and pungent than pepper.

ELECAMPANE: an aromatic bitter plant, formerly regarded as an expectorant. Also a coarse candy, professedly made from the root of the plant, but really composed of little else than coloured sugar.

ERINGO, ERYNGO: sea holly. Its roots were formerly candied as a sweetmeat, and were believed to possess strong aphrodisiacal properties.

FEVERFEW: Pyrethrum Parthenium, which has tonic and bitter qualities, was supposed to be efficacious against fever, hence the name.

FRIGGISE: fricassee.

GALINGALE: Cyperus longus; originally a synonym of Galanga—a dried rhizome brought from China and used in medicine, being an aromatic stimulant of the nature of ginger.

GUM-ARABIC: the gum or juice of various species of trees of the genus Acacia (popularly called mimosa) hardened in the air. It is collected chiefly in north-east Africa, occurring in small, round or spheroidal tears. It is sometimes used as a demulcent, but more generally as a mere adhesive.

GUM DRAGAUNT: gum-tragacanth. A gum yielded by several eastern species of Astragalus, of the sub-genus Tragacantha.

HOLLAND: a kind of fine linen formerly made in Holland; also a coarser linen fabric for covering carpets, furniture, etc.

HOOP: a quart-pot, so called because it was formerly bound with hoops like a barrel.

HORSE-SPICE: for the ingredients of this see N.B. ΦΙΛΙΠΠΟΣ, *The Farrier's and Horseman's Dictionary*, London, 1726, pp. 282-3.

INCLE, INKLE: a brass wheel, with a jagged or notched edge, for cutting cakes into ornamental figures.

JOHN-APPLE: a sort of apple good for spring use, when all other fruit has been used up, as it long retains its freshness.

LABDANUM, LADANUM: the resinous juice of Cistus ladaniferus (Spain and Portugal), and of Cistus creticus (Crete, Syria, etc.). It was chiefly used in external applications.

LAWN: here means a sort of fine linen or cambric.

LIMBECK: to strain or pass through a still; to distil.

LIMBER: pliant, flexible, yielding.

LOAF-SUGAR: sugar refined and formed into a conical mass.

MACE: a fragrant spice.

MALAGAS: probably Malaga raisins.

MANCHET: a small loaf of pure white bread.

MANUS CHRISTI: in 1706 defined as 'Refined sugar boil'd with Rose-water, or that of Violets, or Cinamon; a sort of Cordial for very weak Persons'.

MARCHPANE, MARZIPAN: a kind of sweet bread or biscuit; a spice-cake composed of sugar, nuts, pineapple or almonds.

METHEGLIN: a liquor made of honey and water boiled and fermented, often enriched with spices.

MURREY: mulberry, the colour of mulberry.

MUSCARDINE (properly MUSCADINE): several kinds of sweet and strong Italian and French wines, white and red.

NEAT'S TONGUES: ox tongues.

PINION: the joint of a fowl's wing remotest from the body.

PIP: a disease of fowls forming a scale on the tongue.

PURSLAND: purslane, portulaca; used as a herb.

QUODENY: quiddany, quidney. A thick fruit-syrup or jelly; originally and properly made from quinces.

RACE OF GINGER: root of ginger.

RATTEFEA: ratafia, a fine spirituous liquor flavoured with the kernels of several kinds of fruits, particularly cherries, apricots and peaches.

ROSA SOLIS: sundew. Nicholas Culpeper, in *The English Physitian enlarged*, London, 1666, p. 209, writes: 'Rosa Solis, or Sun-dew. Rosa Solis is accounted good to help those that have salt Rhewm distilling on the Lungs, which breedeth a Consumption, and therefore the distilled water thereof in Wine, is held fit and profitable for such to drink, which Water will be of a Gold yellow colour. The same Water is held to be good for all other diseases of the lungs, as Phtisicks, Wheesings, shortness of breath, or the Cough; as also to heal the Ulcers that happen in the Lungs, and it comforteth the Heart and fainting Spirits.'

ROSE-WATER: water tinctured with roses by distillation.

RUNDLE: probably for rundlet, the same as runlet.

RUNLET: a small barrel, usually containing about 15 gallons.

SAUNDERS: sanders, sandalwood. There is a red variety called red sanders. Cochineal and saunders were both used to colour dishes red.

SCORCINARY: scorzonera, a plant much cultivated in Europe for its root, which is used as a vegetable and somewhat resembles the parsnip. S. Hispanica = black salsify, formerly called viper's-grass. It was thought to be effective against the bites of vipers and other venomous creatures.

SEARCE, SEARSE: to sift, to separate the fine part from the coarse.

SHEARD: presumably = shread, shred.

SILLABUB, SYLLABUB: a dish made by mixing wine or cider with cream or milk, thus forming a soft curd.

SINOR: probably for sinow = sinew.

SIPPET: a small piece of bread or toast usually put in soup.

SKILLET: a small vessel of iron, copper, or other metal, with a long handle, used for heating and boiling water and other culinary purposes.

SLIP-COAT CHEESE: a rich variety of cheese made from milk warm from the cow, and resembling butter, but white.

SPERMACETI: a fatty material obtained chiefly from cavities in the skull of the whale *Physeter*. It is an oily white liquid, and has considerable nutritive qualities when taken internally. Externally it is used in ointments.

STEANE, STEEN: a vessel of clay or stone.

STIVE: to stuff, cram; to stew, as meat.

STROKINGS: the last milk drawn from a cow, 'afterings'. In 1844 the afterings or strokings were 'well known to be the richest part of the milk'. In E. Smith's *The Compleat Housewife* (third edition, 1729) we find that 'to make the Queen's cheese you take six quarts of the best Stroakings, and let them stand till they are cold'.

TRED: tread, the germinating point on the yolk of an egg.

VERJUICE: an acid liquor expressed from crab-apples, unripe grapes, etc., used for culinary purposes.

VIRGA AUREA: golden rod.

WIG: a bun or small cake made of fine flour.

WORK, TO: to ferment.